# Muhammad Ali

Colleen Hord

rourkeeducationalmedia.com

Teacher Notes available at
rem4teachers.com

www.rourkeeducationalmedia.com

PHOTO CREDITS: Cover, title page, page7 - 10, 12 - 22: © AP Images; page 5: © mauro grigolb; page 6: © Michael Flippo;

Edited by: Precious McKenzie

Cover and interior design by: Renee Brady

**Library of Congress PCN Data**

Muhammad Ali / Colleen Hord (Little World Biographies)
ISBN 978-1-61810-152-5 (hard cover)(alk. paper)
ISBN 978-1-61810-285-0 (soft cover)
ISBN 978-1-61810-409-0 (e-Book)
Library of Congress Control Number: 2011945878

Rourke Educational Media
Printed in the United States of America,
North Mankato, Minnesota

rourkeeducationalmedia.com
customerservice@rourkeeducationalmedia.com • PO Box 643328 Vero Beach, Florida 32964

# Table of Contents

# The Stolen Bike

Have you ever had something stolen? When Muhammad Ali was twelve years old, he had his bike stolen. He told a police officer he wanted to fight the person who took his bike.

The police officer was also a manager of a boxing club. He told Muhammad if he was going to fight someone he had better know how. He offered to teach him how to box at his club.

*Muhammad Ali at age 12.*

He helped Muhammad get over being angry about his bike, and taught him how to box.

# Boxing Career

Muhammad became a very good boxer because he trained very hard. He was determined to become a champion. By 1960, he was in the **Olympics** and won the Gold Medal for the United States.

*Muhammad Ali's 1960 Summer Olympic win launched his famous boxing career.*

He soon became the world's boxing light heavyweight champion. Muhammad was famous all over the world.

# Vietnam War

Although Muhammad was famous, some people did not agree with him when he refused to fight in the Vietnam War.

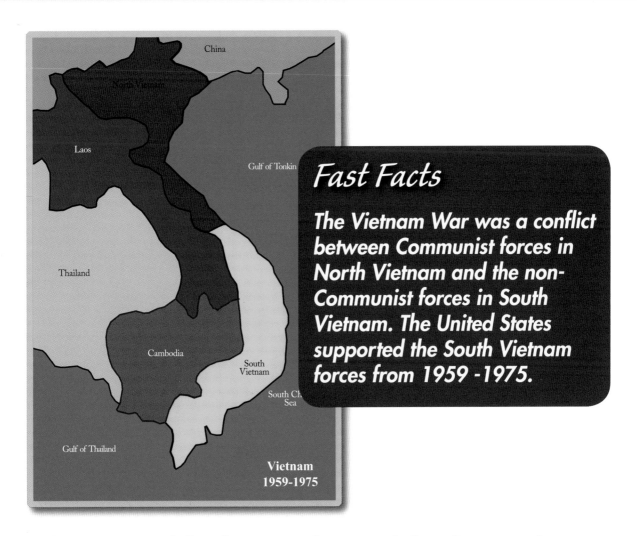

**Vietnam
1959-1975**

Muhammad belonged to a black Muslim religious group. Muhammad's religious belief was that it was wrong for him to go to war.

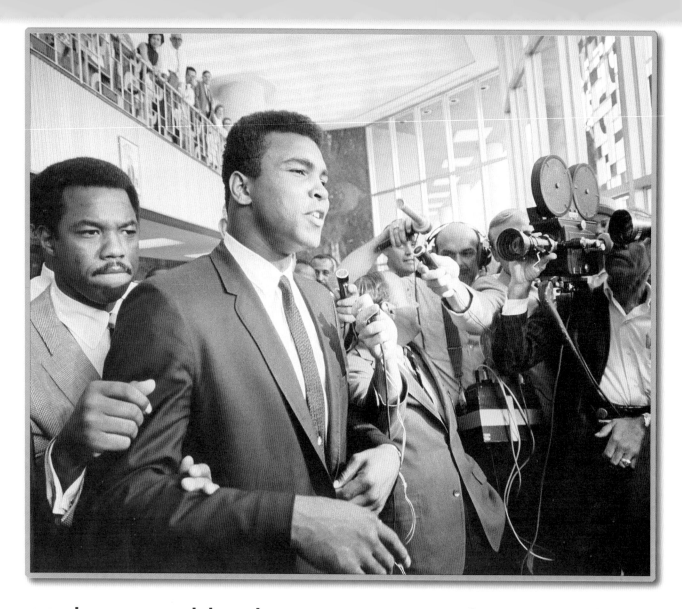

Muhammad had to go to court because he would not join the **armed forces**.

Some people thought he was **unpatriotic**.

# Return to the Ring

The World Boxing Association took away his championship title because of his politics. He was not allowed to box for three years.

*Muhammad Ali and Oscar Bonavena boxing at Madison Square Garden, New York City on December 7, 1970.*

In 1970, he returned to the ring and continued boxing.

*Muhammad Ali and George Foreman. Ali won the heavyweight title back from Foreman on October 30, 1974.*

Muhammad won many fights and regained his title. Once again, he was the heavyweight champion.

*Muhammad Ali reads one his famous pre-fight poems, 1974.*

*"Float like a butterfly, sting like a bee.*
*His hands can't hit what his eyes can't see.*
*Now you see me, now you don't.*
*George thinks he will, but I know he won't."*

*- Muhammad Ali, 1964*

# End of Boxing Career

*Muhammad Ali and his then wife, Veronica, announced his diagnosis at a press conference in New York on September 21, 1984.*

In 1984, he told the public that he had **Parkinson's** disease and he had to quit boxing.

*At the 1996 Summer Olympics in Atlanta, Muhammad Ali lit the cauldron to open the games.*

Muhammad did not let his illness stop him. He wanted to make a difference in the world.

# Fighting Poverty

Muhammad Ali decided to use his **fame** and money to fight **poverty** and promote peace.

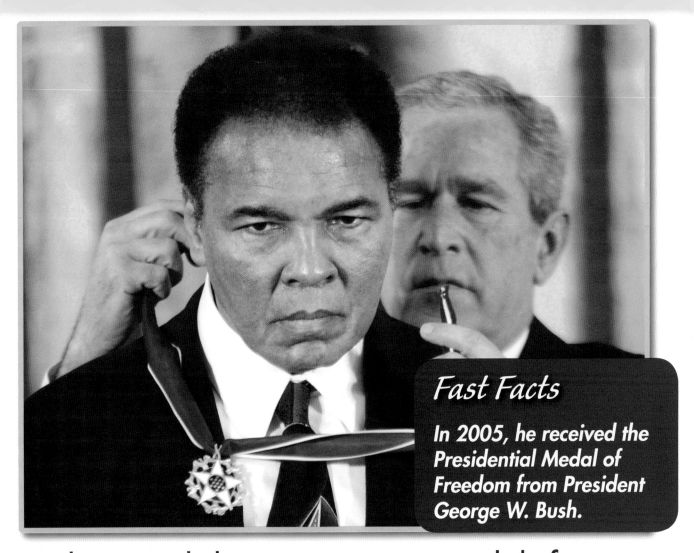

Muhammad does not receive medals for boxing anymore, but he does receive medals for helping people all over the world.

## Timeline

| | |
|---|---|
| 1942 | Cassius Clay, Jr. born (January 17) |
| 1960 | World Light Heavyweight Champion at the Olympics |
| 1984 | Announces his diagnosis with Parkinson's |
| 2005 | Awarded Presidential Medal of Freedom |

# Glossary

**armed forces** (ARMD FORS-ez): all of the branches of a country's military like the Army and Navy

**fame** (FAYM): being well known

**Olympics** (oh-LIM-piks): competition in summer and winter sports held every four years for athletes from all over the world

**Parkinson's** (PAR-kin-suhnz): an incurable disease causing tremors and involuntary movements

**poverty** (POV-ur-tee): the state of being poor

**unpatriotic** (uhn-PAY-tree-ah-tik): not showing love for your country

# Index

# Websites

www.sikids.com

www.alicenter.org

www.lii.org

# About the Author

Colleen Hord is an elementary teacher. Her favorite part of her teaching day is Writer's Workshop. She enjoys kayaking, camping, walking on the beach, and reading in her hammock.

Ask The Author!
www.rem4students.com